James Laughlin Hughes

How to Secure and Retain Attention

Volume 1

James Laughlin Hughes

How to Secure and Retain Attention
Volume 1

ISBN/EAN: 9783337285883

Printed in Europe, USA, Canada, Australia, Japan

Cover: Foto ©Andreas Hilbeck / pixelio.de

More available books at **www.hansebooks.com**

W. J. Gage & Co.'s Manuals for Teachers.

HOW TO
SECURE AND RETAIN
ATTENTION.

BY

JAMES L. HUGHES,

Inspector of Public Schools, Toronto, Canada.

"Attention makes the genius; all learning, fancy and science depend upon it."

SECOND EDITION.

W. J. GAGE & CO., TORONTO, CANADA.
W. KENT & CO., PATERNOSTER ROW, LONDON, ENGLAND.
A. S. BARNES & CO., NEW YORK, U.S.

Entered according to Act of Parliament of Canada in the year 1880 by W. J. GAGE & COMPANY, in the office of the Minister of Agriculture.

PREFACE.

" There is and there can be no teaching, where the attention of the scholar is not secured. The teacher who fails to get the attention of his scholars, fails totally." So writes a thoughtful educator, and every observant teacher knows that the statements are correct. The most important work of a teacher both in regard to the learning of school lessons and the formation of proper mental habits by his pupils, is the development of the power to give concentrated and sustained attention to a subject.

While fully agreeing with the opinion that natural aptitude has much to do in deciding the measure of a teacher's success, the author knows that the power of securing and retaining attention can be acquired and developed. This book has been written with a sincere desire to aid in the accomplishment of this important object.

TORONTO, February 20th, 1880.

CONTENTS.

Chap.		Page
I.	Kinds of Attention	1
II.	Characteristics of Positive Attention	4
III.	Characteristics of the Teacher in securing and retaining Attention	19
IV.	Conditions of Attention	23
V.	How to control a class	29
VI.	Method of preserving and stimulating the pupils' desire for knowledge	36
VII.	How to gratify and develop the natural desire for mental activity	48
VIII.	The cultivation of the Senses	62
IX.	General Suggestions	75

HOW TO SECURE AND RETAIN ATTENTION.

CHAPTER I.

KINDS OF ATTENTION.

Attention may be *Negative* or *Positive*.

Negative Attention. A pupil may look without seeing, listen without being conscious of hearing, and hear without comprehending. He may sit and dream. The mind has *inner* as well as *outer* gates. The outer gates admit merely to the courtyard of the mind. A great many pupils keep the inner doors closed to much of the teaching done by their teachers. We may perceive without receiving distinct conceptions. Thousands look at a store window in passing it without being able to name or even give the color of a single article in it.

We may hear also without taking in the thoughts of the person speaking. How often men sit in church and hear a preacher's voice without noting his words! The sounds he makes get through the gates of the castle wall, but the castle itself is shut and filled with other tenants. The telephonic key has not been adjusted, and direct communication has not been established. We hear various sounds—the bell of the factory or the school, the whistle of the steam engine, the song of the birds, &c.—without always being consciously impressed by them. Sometimes they influence or arrest our lines of thought, but more frequently, unless they convey a special message to us, we allow them to pass unheeded. Negative attention consists in the outward marks of attention merely. It is a form without reality; a seed without an active germ, from which nothing of life and beauty can ever spring.

Positive Attention. A pupil who gives positive or *active* attention, is attentive not merely with his body but with his mind. He has the *inner* as well as the outer gates of his mind open. His mind must be *willing* to receive the thoughts his teacher has to communicate, and it must not be preoccupied, or *actively engaged with*

KINDS OF ATTENTION.

other thoughts. He must for a time forget his personality, and turn from thoughts of his own plays and work and all that directly interests him outside of the lesson. He must get out of his own current of thought and into that of his teacher.

Positive attention stands opposed to that rambling state of mind in which the thoughts move continually from one topic to another without dwelling upon any; and also to that apathetic and listless condition of the mind in which it is not conscious of thought; or in which ideas, if they exist, leave no trace in the memory. It is the kind of attention which a teacher must have from his pupils if he wishes to impress them. If he secures only *negative*, the minds of his scholars may be a thousand miles away, whilst their bodies may occupy positions of reverent attention.

CHAPTER II.

CHARACTERISTICS OF POSITIVE ATTENTION.

1. Positive attention may be either instinctive or controlled.

Instinctive attention. Attention may be won or directed, attracted or guided. Pupils may give attention to a subject because they are interested in it, or because they are convinced that they will receive benefit from so attending. We attend to many things without effort, and even in opposition to our wishes. Those things which give us either pleasure or pain demand and receive our attention in proportion to the intensity of the interest they have for us. The little child gives attention because it is a delight to do so. It attends to one thing until another becomes more attractive. "Observation, attention, concentration, last so long as enjoyment lasts and no longer." The mind of the little one flies like the bee from flower to flower, and it gets something every time it alights. The child does not pass from object to object for the sake of information however, but on account of the beauty and attractiveness of the things themselves. Nevertheless it gathers the knowledge more easily and more rapidly than it ever does afterwards, even when the acquisition of knowledge is its direct object. The child learns more between the ages of two and a half and four years' than it does during any five years afterwards. He has learned a language, and speaks it correctly both as regards grammar and pronunciation, if he has listened to good speaking. He is intimately acquainted with the worlds of nature and of art so far as he has come in contact with them. He knows the relations of things to each other and to himself. He cannot explain, but he puts in practice the principles of philosophy. He is even capable to a far greater extent than he usually gets credit for, of estimating and appreciating the motives as well as the actions of the adults by whom he is surrounded.

He could not have learned thus rapidly, if it had not been for the power of *instinctive* attention, the intensity of which in a child is so great as to require but a short time to gather ideas. Teachers will do well to note carefully, not only the marvellous rapidity with which knowledge is acquired in early years, but the distinctness and permanency of ideas received in the days of childhood. Many parents and teachers complain of the flightiness of children, and their lack of continuity in giving fixed attention to a subject. If these wise grumblers would only reflect, they would find that this tendency to pay attention to whatever gives the highest degree of joy or pain is a characteristic of childhood impressed by our Creator. The results already noted clearly prove that it is not necessary to give long continued so much as oft repeated attention to a subject in order to become acquainted with it. The clearness and permanency of ideas depends on the *interest* and *intensity* of attention rather than its continuance. If the best teachers could only succeed in making children learn one half as rapidly during school days as they did in their homes or in the fields and woods before school life began, they would have great reason to congratulate themselves.

Why do children not continue to manifest the same degree of interested or instinctive attention through life, that they showed in early years? Is the change due to an altered mental nature, or is it caused by improper methods of teaching? Partly to both, but mainly to the latter. Professor Payne says, "It is certain, that there are processes of so-called education in vogue amongst us which, by the assiduous cultivation of mere rote memory, convert teaching into a mechanical grind of words, and thus defeat the very aim of true education, which is to store the mind with ideas, and only to recognize words as far as they minister to this end. The lamentable results of such methods which make much provision for feeding and none for digestion is *to ruin irreparably the appetite for knowledge*—the knowledge which consists in ideas not words. Hence it is that we see children, who in their earliest years were distinguished for mental ability transformed into dunces at school—a consequence obviously due to what is miscalled their education; for the number of children really stupid by nature is probably not at all greater than that of those born blind, or deaf and dumb."

There is one fundamental difference between the natural method and the school method of teaching, which is worthy of careful thought by teachers. Before school the learning has not been the direct object aimed at. It has been *incidental*. The child was attracted by something, and he watched it, or handled it, or used it, in order to add to his happiness. He was not attending to lessons merely, but he learned them thoroughly, as the result of his doing. School work cannot all be done on this principle, but it should be done so as far as possible. There will be enough "drudgery" under the most favorable circumstances to serve for mental discipline.

Frœbel in his Kindergarten system has sought to utilize the *instinctive* attention of children to the fullest extent. He recognizes the immense rapidity and value of the development of even the infant mind, and sets to work with the idea of systematizing the child's work without in any sense curtailing his enjoyment. He consequently brings him in contact with a carefully graded series of objects and occupations which are most attractive to him, and at the same time are admirably suited to the growth of his observant and reflective powers. He also allows him to have ample opportunity for unrestrained but directed play. There are some who, having merely *glanced* theoretically or practically at the surface of Kindergarten work, wisely express the opinion that it is "only play." It is scarcely honest for a man to give oracular decisions with such a small amount of investigation. There would not be much gold in the Kindergarten system, if a casual and unprofessional observer could find it all in a few minutes. The truth is that the Kindergarten system, by extending the period of *instinctive, involuntary attention*, has done a great deal towards the bridging over of the great gulf between the home and the school. What is needed in addition is the strengthening and completion of the bridge at its school end. In some subjects the Kindergarten system should be carried out even in universities.

Controlled Attention. Bain says, "The beginnings of knowledge are in activity or in pleasure, but the culminating point is in the power of attending to things *in themselves indifferent.*" It must not be forgotten that while *instinctive* or *attracted* attention is the most effective kind in gaining knowledge, *controlled* or *directed* attention is of more importance as a mental discipline. All studies cannot be made so attractive that students will prosecute them with ardor on account of the delight they afford. Different minds are fond of studying different subjects. Study may be a species of mental dissipation. As children grow older therefore, they should be introduced gradually to those subjects which are less attractive. The mistake that is too often made in both public and Sunday schools is to expect young children to attend to the teaching of subjects to which they are *indifferent.* To do this requires the exercise of a will power which they do not possess. Dr. Carpenter expresses himself very clearly on this point. He says, "Those strongminded teachers who object to these modes of 'making things pleasant' as an unworthy and undesirable 'weakness' are ignorant that in this stage of the child-mind, the *will,* that is the power of *self control,* is weak, and that the primary object of education is to encourage and strengthen, not to repress that power * * To punish a child for the want of obedience which it has not the power to render, is to inflict an injury which may almost be said to be irreparable."

It will not do on the other hand to allow the child to grow up with the idea that none of the problems of life are uninviting in themselves. The teacher should fit his pupils for grappling with and mastering difficulties, even with what is distasteful. One of the most important of all the mental powers is the will; and it must be called into action in fixing the attention to these subjects that cannot be made attractive. "God has given us the power or capacity to direct the mind to any given object—that is, of directing, controlling, and in any way using the several mental faculties of which we are possessed: just as we have a like power over the various members of the body." Let this power be developed, but let the teacher carefully avoid depending upon compulsory attention as a substitute for good teaching.

2. Positive attention is a "result of good

teaching rather than a condition on which the power to teach well depends." Those effeminate or fossilized teachers who weakly say "Oh, dear! If my pupils would only *give* me their attention, I could teach them so well," should honestly say, "If I taught better, my class would attend to my teaching."

3. Positive attention cannot be secured by demanding it, or by coaxing, scolding, commanding, threatening, or reasoning. The maxim, "One man may lead a horse to the water, but ten men cannot *make* him drink," applies with great force here. *Negative* attention may be secured by compulsion, *positive* cannot be *forced*. We can force order, and submission, but not *active* attention. It must be willingly given. He who demands something entirely beyond the limits of his control, demonstrates his own weakness and presumption. Coaxing, scolding, commanding and threatening very soon lose their influence, and, if indulged in after that point has been reached, they secure for the teachers who use them the disrespect of their pupils. Even reasoning with pupils cannot permanently secure attention. It will certainly be of service for the teacher to show his pupils clearly the necessity for attention, and the benefits arising from it. This will produce in them a mental attitude favorable to attention, and will thereby make it easier for them to do their part, but it does not relieve the teacher of his responsibility for sustaining the interest in the lesson.

4. Positive attention should be undivided. Some children have difficulty in concentrating their attention. Their minds do not merely pass rapidly from one thing to another; two or three subjects of an entirely different nature will occupy them at the same time. It is possible for a man to give his attention to two things at once, but the attention given to one of them is taken from the other. It is one of the highest duties which a teacher owes to his pupils to train them to be able to fix their undivided attention on one subject. The extent to which a man can rivet his attention, and control the working of his own mind, decides the standard of his intellectual power. The force of a stream becomes resistless as its channel becomes restricted. The genial rays of the sun when brought to a focus have intense burning power.

The mind which admits various subjects at the same time, and as a result becomes confused and full of but indistinct ideas, might, if all its energies were directed to the investigation of only one subject, mount with majestic tread from height to height in original investigation.

It is a difficult matter, however, even for adults to concentrate their attention on the one subject in hand. How often the thoughts which we hear expressed, or which we read, make no deeper impressions on our minds than the " shadows of the passing clouds do upon a landscape." A teacher should be patient when he finds some active brained boy or girl is in "wonder-land," when he is supposed to be revelling in the delights of complex fractions. It is often injurious to a very young child to startle it from its reveries. Mental links may thus be broken which will never be re-united. This remark should, however, be noted by parents and teachers of individuals, rather than by teachers of classes.

5. **Positive attention should be intense.**

The permanency of impressions made upon the mind by the teacher or by circumstances depends upon the intensity of the attention given. Some single events have burned their impress upon the tablets of our memory, so that they can never be forgotten. It matters not whether the circumstances have caused intense joy or pain, if the sensations they caused have been acute, their remembrance remains vivid. There are few who would not forget some things, *if they could*. Why is it that we cannot forget some things? Simply because they interested us so much. We walk through the streets of a city and we look into the faces of thousands of strangers. Why is it that of all these perhaps but one is photographed indelibly in our remembrance? Because it reminded us of some other person closely connected with our lives by the links of love or hate, or because for some reason it strongly attracted or repelled us. We look at and admire the beautiful flowers which bloom around our pathway as we ramble in the woods or gardens in the early summer time. We perchance may gather bouquets of those we deem most exquisitely beautiful. A month afterwards we may not remember the varieties we collected or the precise localities in the woods or gardens from which we plucked them. Let a companion who has roused in us a strong deep feeling either of love or respect, pick and present one blossom to us, and we remember exactly its hues and shape, as well as the very spot on which the presentation took place. Numerous other illustrations might be given, were they necessary to show that when the attention is *intense*, the impressions made are distinct and lasting.

Teachers should therefore strive to secure a large degree of intensity of attention on the part of their pupils. This may not be possible in every part of every lesson, but there should at least be some part of every lesson which will arrest the involuntary attention of every pupil. If only one flower be clearly pictured in the memory, that one serves to recall the ramble and its pleasures. If some salient or culminating point in a lesson be illustrated, or presented in an impressive or even startling manner so as to condense the attention on it, it will form a magnet around which the other facts taught will group themselves. Bain says: " Intensity of sensation whether pleasing or not is a power." Of course it would be unwise to try to keep the attention constantly strained to too great an extent. The effects of such a course both physically and mentally would be disastrous.

6. Positive attention should be fixed.
Startling a class to make them attend is not a wise course. Some teachers try an explosive method of securing attention. They first helplessly allow the class to drift into a state of disorder and confusion, and then suddenly comes a thunderclap; the desk is struck violently with a ruler, or the floor is stamped upon heavily. Attention may be gained in such a way, but only of a *temporary* kind. The noise of the pupils yields for a time, but very soon it reasserts itself. Attention to be valuable must be *fixed*. Teachers should, of course, never forget that giving fixed, active attention is an *exhaustive* exercise, and that relaxation in some form—music, free gymnastics, or both combined—should be given to pupils at frequent intervals.

The attention which the teacher should try to secure should therefore be:
1. **Active.**
2. **Instinctive** or **Controlled;** if possible the former. It should be *won* rather than *forced*.
3. **Willingly given.**
4. **Undivided.**
5. **Intense.**
6. **Fixed.**

CHAPTER III.

CHARACTERISTICS OF THE TEACHER ESSENTIAL IN SECURING AND RETAINING ATTENTION.

1. Cheerfulness. Unless the teacher be cheerful and kind in manner he cannot secure the *sympathy* of his pupils thoroughly, and without it he cannot obtain proper attention. The pupils insensibly associate the teacher with the subjects taught, and unless attracted by the former they are not likely to be interested in the latter.

2. Earnestness. The teacher's manner will influence his pupils for good more than his precepts or advice. They may laugh at his logic, they cannot resist his personal power. If a man is not in earnest his pupils will not be zealous. He justifies inattention, if he does not speak and act in such a way as to show that he regards his subjects to be of great importance.

3. Enthusiasm. Enthusiasm is well directed energy, not mere excitement or assumed animation. Enthusiasm must spring from a genuine fervent desire for the accomplishment of a well understood purpose. Enthusiasm in teaching must grow from a love for the work, a thorough acquaintance with the subjects to be taught, and a deep conviction of the great value of education in forming the characters and securing the success of his pupils. Some one says, " Enthusiastic men are narrow." Perhaps they are to a certain extent, but narrowing a man's energies to his legitimate work is the most essential foundation for his success. The teacher should *widen* his mental range, and *concentrate his energies and his emotional nature.* " Enthusiasm is not a reckless zeal without knowledge ; neither is it that overplus of feeling or action that *over*does the work, but *un*does the worker. But it does consist in the combination of a high appreciation of the importance of your work, and a hearty zeal in the accomplishment of that work. Fanaticism is zeal without knowledge ; indifference is no zeal whatever ; enthusiasm is a zeal tempered by prudence, modified by knowledge. Indifference chills; enthusiasm warms and quickens. A teacher without enthusiasm has no right to be a teacher. He cannot be one in the truest and broadest sense without it."

4. Quietness. Some teachers act as though noise and bustle were equivalent to energy and enthusiasm. The mighty Corliss Engine in Machinery Hall at the Centennial Exhibition at Philadelphia in 1876, made less noise than almost any of the hundreds of machines which it set in motion. So in the schoolroom, the teacher should be the great motive power, mighty without being noisy, which sets the human machines around him to *work for themselves.* "Noise and emptiness often travel together." Noisy teachers make noisy pupils. Some teachers are so noisy and demonstrative that they attract attention to themselves and not to the subjects they are teaching. If teachers speak in a loud tone, and in a high key their pupils cannot listen to them long. Inattention and consequent disorder always mark the classes taught by piping teachers.

5. Decision. The teacher's every act, look

and tone should clearly indicate decision. He must wear the dignity of his superior position as though it fitted him well. He must understand himself and his subjects. There must be no assumption in his bearing. There is a magnetic force connected with a man who has definiteness of aim and deliberation in action. The will power of such a man is irresistible in its influence over those with whom he comes in contact. This is true even when they are of his own age; it is true to a greater extent when they are his juniors.

6. Power to maintain interest. The teacher must not be too wordy. Fluency often drowns thought. Pupils will not exercise their minds, if the teacher does their thinking for them. The best way to make a subject interesting and attractive is to set the pupils to work at making discoveries concerning it. The wondrous caves and marvellous treasures of knowledge may be opened and pointed out by the teacher, but they should be investigated by the pupils themselves. In some way, however, the interest must be kept up, and as far as possible the subjects taught should be made attractive in themselves, without reference to the benefits they confer. As has been explained already, the permanency of impressions depends upon the intensity of the attention given; it is equally true that intensity of attention depends upon the interest taken in the subject itself.

7. The possession of "will power." Control is a necessary element in securing attention. The most perfect control can secure only *negative* attention, but this is an essential condition of *positive* attention. The teacher should have no difficulty in convincing his class that some *one* person must be the controlling power in the school, and that his age, experience and developed force of character eminently fit him for the position of unchallenged leader. The teacher who, when occasion demands it, has not the power to secure complete submission from his pupils by an arbitrary use of "will power" is unfit for his position.

CHAPTER IV.

CONDITIONS OF ATTENTION.

1. Physical requisites. *The room must be well lighted.* Children cannot be bright and happy in a room that is insufficiently or badly lighted. The light should never come from the front or the right of pupils. It is best when admitted *only from the left,* but a left and rear light is admissible. All windows should reach well up towards the ceiling, and they should not extend too low down. It is better when all the light is admitted above the level of the eye.

2. *The room must be properly ventilated.* Unless it is, the health of the children is injuriously affected, and their spirits are depressed.

3. *The temperature must be regulated.* Pupils cannot be quiet and studious when their toes and

fingers are cold. They become tired and indolent if the temperature rises too high. Cold feet and hot heads at the same time are bad for the health in many respects. The normal temperature is about 65 degrees.

4. *The pupils must be seated comfortably.* The two essentials for comfort are—

1. The seats must not be *too high*.

2. The backs should fit the pupils' spinal curvature.

A child's feet should rest on the floor, so that no part of the weight of the leg is borne by the thigh bone. Many seats have backs too high, others are too low, and sometimes the seats in galleries have no backs at all. Either arrangement is a cause of pain to the children who sit on such seats.

5. *Children should be allowed to change their posture frequently.* The body tires sooner than the mind. Even if supplied with comfortable seats, remaining in one position too long causes injury to the body, and compels the withdrawal of the mind from the lesson, to note the necessities of physical comfort.

If the teacher notices his pupils unusually restless and inattentive, he should allow them to spend say half a minute in some simple physical exercises. Even standing up and sitting down will aid in removing listlessness, and the disorder resulting from nervous restlessness. Exercises should always, if possible, be performed in time with *music*. They then form the most powerful and, what is of more importance, the most *natural* disciplinary agent a teacher can employ.

2. Good classification. Proper classification promotes attention in two ways. Unless the pupils in a class are graded according to their attainments, the subjects and methods adapted to the advancement and capabilities of one portion will be quite unsuited to the other. It is comparatively useless to try to steer a middle course. The more advanced will not give good attention because they think they are acquainted with the subject already, the more backward will usually fail to give close attention from sheer inability to keep up and clearly comprehend the teaching. Judicious grading also enables the teacher to secure a proper alternation of lessons on the programme of study, and to carry out the time table without waste of time.

3. Good Order. Order is an essential preliminary step in securing and retaining attention. Attention cannot be concentrated and intense, except under favorable circumstances. Disorder, unnecessary movement, bustle, confusion, chattering, and even whispering, distracts the attention. Those who talk must themselves be inattentive, and they prevent attention on the part of those to whom they speak. A recent American writer says: "*Silence* is the basis for the culture of internality or reflection—the soil in which thought grows. It allows the repose of the senses and the awakening of insight and reflection. In our schools this is carried further than merely negative silence and the pupil is taught the difficult but essential habit of absorption in his proper task even when a lively recitation is going on with another class. He must acquire the strength of mind (of internality) which will enable him to pursue without distraction his train of thought and study, under any external conditions. Out of this discipline grow attention, memory, thought—the three factors of theoretic culture."

The teacher must carefully guard against the mistake of supposing that order and attention are equivalent. A class may be very orderly, and at the same time in a state of mental inactivity. Order and attention are quite distinct, but closely related to each other. Order is indispensable in *securing* attention; attention is absolutely requisite in *maintaining* order.

4. Full Control. While order should be maintained by giving the pupils plenty of work to engage their attention, it frequently becomes necessary to secure it by direct controlling power. To influence his pupils properly a teacher must first learn to control them. In teaching them to apply themselves to the study of subjects "indifferent," or uninteresting; in forming habits of mental attention for benefit rather than pleasure; in developing the will power of pupils; and the teacher's mind must assume not only a guiding but a governing function. It is of course true that the minds of the pupils may influence that of the teacher, but the extent to which this is true depends almost entirely on the teacher himself. Four things settle the question of mental control between the teacher and the taught.

1. The natural strength of the teacher's mind.

2. His force of character.

3. The interest he takes in his work.

4. The clearness of his conception of the subjects he desires to teach.

The weak, careless, indolent teacher, who has not thoroughly prepared the special lesson he has to teach, will not be a controlling power to a very large extent.

CHAPTER V.

HOW TO CONTROL A CLASS.

It is clear from what has already been said that gaining *control* is a totally different matter from securing *attention*. Attention includes control, however, and it is therefore necessary that a teacher should control his pupils as a basis for obtaining attention from them. This he may do as follows:

1. By standing or sitting so as to see his whole class. If a pupil feels that his teacher's eye is *constantly* and quietly taking note of all that is going on in his class, he cannot fail to be conscious of its controlling power. Unless he is defiant or exceedingly thoughtless he will need little more than the teacher's untiring eye to restrain him. The eye can be cultivated and its range of vision greatly widened. Few teachers have the power to *see* and *watch* every pupil in a class of fifty at the same instant, but every teacher may acquire the ability to do so. It is astonishing to what extent clearness of lateral vision may be developed, without rolling the eyes from side to side. An uneasy, nervous movement of the eyes, or a fixed stare neutralizes the influence they might exert. The seeing should be done without any apparent effort, but it should be, done, and done unerringly. Even when using the blackboard the teacher should avoid turning his back to his class. "The eye has a magic power. It wins, it fascinates, it guides, it rewards, it punishes, it controls. *You must learn how to see* every child all the time."

2. Inattention must be noticed and checked in time. It is an epidemic, which may be easily controlled in its incipient stage. The fire that sweeps away in a breath the proudest structures of a mighty city might have been quenched with a few drops of water. It is madness to allow a wave of disorder to roll on and on until it has engulfed a whole class, and then attempt to break its force by a counter disorder of greater violence. "A stitch in time saves nine" is as true in school as in other places. The inattention of one pupil in a large class, if of such a negative character as not to attract the attention of others, sometimes may be allowed to pass unnoticed. It may cost too much to secure the attention of such a pupil. The whole class may be diverted from the subject under consideration in doing so, and a positive evil substituted for a negative. The class should not be sacrificed for the individual. He may be informed at the close of the lesson, or before passing to a new line of thonght, that his negligence has been noticed. This will soon cure him, and it will at the same time impress the rest of the class with the idea that the teacher regards their attention as of such vital importance as to avoid allowing anything unnecessarily to interrupt it. They will learn the importance of giving attention from his actions and manner more clearly than from his words. But as soon as passive inattention develops into the first symptoms of disorder, action must be taken instantly. How should this action be taken? In the quietest possible manner. The cure of the affected portion should be made without injury to any other part. If the teacher's object is to startle the whole class and completely dissipate their attention from the subject in hand, he should scold the offender or strike the desk, or stamp on the floor, or snappishly demand "attention." If he wishes to gain the attention of the careless pupil without allowing any one else to know that he has been inattentive, he can usually do so in one of the following ways:

1. By briefly pausing in the lesson.

2. By a quiet movement of the hand or head.

3. By a significant glance.

4. By giving a question to the wandering one.

With a fair degree of tact the remedy may be applied without loss of time to any but the pupil immediately concerned.

It is very desirable that the class should be saved from interruptions by the teacher himself. The interruptions referred to are the worst possible, for they not only cause loss of time and distraction of attention, but they lead the whole class to believe that inattention is a very common, and therefore not a very grave offence.

3. By calm, fixed, fearless, determined, patient "will power." Every teacher should exercise "will power" in relation to his class. It should never be exercised haughtily or tyrannically, but always kindly and naturally. Wilfulness and self-will are very different from "will power." "Will power" simply means the ability to proceed undeviatingly to a desired end, and bring others along with you. The following are the characteristics which "will power" should possess:

1. *It should be calm.* Obedience on any terms is better than disobedience, but willing obedience must be secured by the teacher if he wishes to benefit his pupils. If "will power" is exerted in a noisy or violent manner it is offensive; if it is of the fussy kind it excites ridicule. It must

be calm if it would secure control, beneath the placid surface of which no rebellion lurks in ambush.

2. *It should be fixed.* Some teachers are intermittent in their exercise of "will power." They are fully charged with energy and force one day, but seem to have lost connection with their character batteries on the next. Steady, even, regular, uniform control is the kind required. In the schoolroom and in the yard the teacher's influence should be supreme, whether he is present or absent. He must never be a tyrant, he should always be a governor.

3. *It should be fealress.* No one can control a pupil if he fears him or his parents. The teacher should carefully study his proper social and legal relationship to the pupils, their parents, and the school authorities. He should stand on a foundation of solid rock, and be ready for prompt action in cases of emergency. Promptness and deliberation should go hand in hand. Promptitude and haste or excitement are not synonymous. Hesitation and timidity on the part of a teacher often stir to life germs of rebellion which might otherwise have been left to die for lack of nutriment.

4. *It should be determined.* While a teacher should always pay due respect and attention to the advice of friends, he should never allow either the counsel of his friends or the opposition of foes to make him deviate from the course which he knows to be the right and just one. Many men fail because when a wave of opposition meets them they feebly yield to its power and aimlessly drift with it; when if they had met it bravely and remained firm it would soon have passed them and left them better for its washing. The teacher may yield many times with profit to his school and to himself if he does it gracefully, but he can never do so when the question of control is at stake. He must then assert his "will power" in a most determined manner, without making himself offensive or being tyrannical.

5. *It must be patient.* This is the great requisite. The quality of "will power" is of great importance, the quantity of it at a teacher's disposal is of far more consequence. It must wear well. There is a dignity and a majesty in the patient assertion of the right and ability to control, which never fails to command respect. It is well, especially when taking charge of a new class, not to try to compel absolute order too

suddenly. So long as pupils are really trying to do what the teacher wishes, he will, if a reasonable man, overlook slight offences until good conduct has become a habit.

Control asserts itself chiefly through the *lip*, the *tongue* and the *eye*. They should be used in the inverse order to that in which they are named. The eye should be the exclusive medium of control, so far as possible; the tongue may be called to its aid in cases of emergency; the lip should be used very sparingly. The lip expresses firmness, combined with scorn or contempt, and these are sure to stir up active antagonism, rather than submission. A pupil may be, and often is, forced to yield without full obedience. The eye alone can convey a message of power and conciliation at the same time, and these are the elements of genuine control.

However good a teacher's control may be, he must not think that he has secured the attention of his class merely on that account.

CHAPTER VI.

METHODS OF PRESERVING AND STIMULATING THE PUPILS' DESIRE FOR KNOWLEDGE.

Some one calls a child an "Interrogative machine." Truly the appetite for knowledge with which nature endows him is a keen one, and difficult to satisfy. Some writers maintain that it is the duty of the school to set the child going mentally, that he may be self educative when he leaves school. If pupils left school in as self educative a condition as they enter it, there would be less ground for complaint than at pesent. The boy begins to " go " when very young, and for a few years he continues to develop at a very rapid rate. Very few children are dull when very young. Most children make remarkable progress until they go to school. Then too often comes a period of stagnation from which many never emerge. Improper methods are too often the cause of the discouraging change. The following are points deserving consideration by teachers of primary classes.

1. The transition from the home to the school should be less sudden.

The child on entering an ordinary school, passes from comparative freedom to confinement and restraint; from bounding activity to wearisome quiet; from actual things to uninteresting abstractions; from living flowers, and birds, and pets to mere black marks called letters, in which for themselves he can have no active interest; from play to work; from instinctive to compulsory attention; from fresh air and sunshine to bad ventilation and imperfect and often injurious lighting; from the mossy bank to the hard and illformed seat.

Where the Kindergarten can be introduced it serves to make the steps gradual in the change from the home to the school. The school should learn many lessons yet from the home and the Kindergarten. Teachers must study the child more before he enters school, and they should continue in school more closely, the methods of self-education practised by him, while he was at liberty to follow nature's guidance.

2. Knowledge should be used as it is acquired.
Children delight in coming in contact with things which they can use. They care for what a thing does. This shows itself very early in life. The baby learning to talk, names the domestic animals according to the sounds they make. He calls the dog " bow-wow," and the cat " meow." This is true whether the name of the animal is more or less difficult to say than the sound made. While they have been making such rapid strides in learning and mental development at home, they were doing so by handling the things around them and by using their knowledge as quickly as they gained it. What a change comes when they go to school! Many even of the thoughtful class of teachers deliberately reverse this plan. They reason somewhat in this manner; " These children can not do much actual work yet and so we may as well save time by making them do the *drudgery* of school work now." They are therefore set to learn all the letters, before they begin to read, all the tables before they put them to any practical use &c. It is probable that

the letters and the multiplication table have done more to stupify boys and girls than any other causes. Girls and boys can work, and by working they not only learn how to work better, but become familiar with the elements of work they may be using. Even if the worst of all methods of teaching the names of words, the *alphabetic*, be used, no letters should be taught at first but those used on the first page or tablet of *reading* in the primer. The child should *use* the multiplication table, for instance, as he *learns* it, and he will thus pleasantly learn it as he uses it. Using and learning go hand in hand. Practical application is the highest and most effective style of review. A pupil will learn the "Two" line as far as "twice 4" in four minutes, but it will probably forget it in an hour, unless it is allowed to apply the knowledge it has gained. Why not teach it the process of multiplying at once in five minutes more and then set it at work? "Oh, the child should never multiply until it knows its multiplication table!" says some driller. Does the study of the multiplication table qualify a child for the comprehension of the multiplying process? Certainly not. Then again, the child who has been taught as far as "twice four" *does* know the multiplication table, so far as he is required to put it in practice. His teacher can assign several examples with no other multiplier but 2, and no figures in the multiplicand but 1, 2, 3, and 4. It will do him great good to work the very same examples over a second or third time. Next day advancement should be made in the table and much practice given on both lessons, and so on to the end. This method will not prove a source of horror to pupils, but will delight them because they use the information as they get it.

If an apprentice on entering a machine shop, were compelled by the foreman to spend months in learning the names of the various machines, and their different parts, their relations to each other, their uses, &c., would such a course fit him to take charge of even one of the machines? The probability is, that long before the expiration of the time specified his work of learning, at first fascinating to him, would become loathsome, and from loss of interest, he would be to a large degree incapacitated for the highest degree of success in his work. He should, and in charge of a practical man in any department of work, he does begin with the simplest of all the tools or machines, and ne learns how to use it by using it. Others are entrusted to his charge when he is ready for them. Teachers should also be reasonable in familiarizing their pupils with the tools they have to use. The letters, the tables, rules in grammar and other subjects, are merely the tools with which the child should be taught to educate himself, and they should be given to him only as he is able to use them.

3. The work of school should afford pleasure. If the desire for knowledge is to be kept alive and vigorous, if it is to survive through the early years of school life, school work must be made attractive. Herbert Spencer says that of all the educational changes taking place, "The most significant is the growing desire to make the acquirement of knowledge pleasurable rather than painful—a desire based on the more or less distinct perception that at *each age the intellectual action which a child likes is a healthful one for it;* and conversely. There is a spreading opinion that the rise of an appetite for any kind of knowledge implies that the unfolding mind has become fit to assimilate it, and needs it for the purposes of growth; and that on the other hand, the disgust felt towards any kind of knowledge is a sign either that it is prematurely presented, or that it is presented in an indigestible form. Hence the efforts to make early education amusing, and all education interesting. * * As a final test by which to judge any plan of culture, should come the question—Does it create a pleasurable excitement in the pupils?" Discard any system of primary instruction, however time honored or in accordance with theory it may be, unless it makes lessons attractive. With the older children the step from *instinctive* to *controlled* attention must be gradually taken.

It is very desirable that teachers should avoid any course of action which will tend to make learning distasteful. If men are to be self educative when they leave school, they should have a love for knowledge; certainly they must not have an aversion to it. Lessons should never be assigned as a punishment. Pupils may be compelled to do after school or at home, work which they have neglected to do at the right time. This is not a punishment for the neglect however, but the performance of a duty which ought to have been done before.

4. School exercises should be varied as much as possible. Of course the programme of studies should be fixed, and the time table adhered to regularly. The plan of presenting a subject should be changed, however. Some new element should be introduced each day. In teaching Geography, for instance, the map may be used one day, blackboard and slates the next, and the sand-box the next; to-day the teacher may point to the places he wishes to have remembered and the pupils find their names, to-morrow he may give the names and they find their positions on the map. The plan should be varied during a single recitation, to a certain extent. So long as variety does not dissipate the attention, there can not be too much of it. Freshness stimulates mental activity, routine deadens it.

5. The child's curiosity should be kept alive. Some pupils are always on the tip-toe of expectation. The teacher who can secure such a condition in his class, is certain to have attentive scholars. Natural aptitude in the teacher has something to do in stimulating the curiosity of pupils. The power to sustain it, however, must be acquired. Pupils will not long seek to be fed with chaff. *The teacher must be prepared* to gratify the appetite which he aims to develop. He *must* be familiar with the subjects he has to teach; he *should* keep well acquainted with all that relates to them in connection with current events. Hart aptly says: "To real, successful teaching, there must be two things, namely, the ability to hold the minds of the children, and the ability to pour into the minds thus presented sound and seasonable instruction. Lacking the latter ability, your pupil goes away with his vessel unfilled; lacking the former, you only pour water on the ground."

6. The lessons given and the subjects taught ought to be adapted to the advancement of the pupils. If lessons are too difficult a child will naturally turn from them, first in disappointment, afterwards with dislike. The subjects should be presented in a manner suited to the ages of the pupils taught. Some of the most interesting studies are rendered permanently obnoxious by improper methods of teaching them to children at first. In teaching grammar, for instance, dry, difficult, and uninteresting rules, with puzzling *exceptions to the general rule,* are memorized and recited, and the teacher (in addition to this outrage) actually deceives the unfortunate and long-suffering pupils by allowing them to believe that such wearisome drudgery is learning grammar. They, of course, in most cases, associate the unpleasant feelings they receive in school with study and learning in the abstract, and therefore get a distaste for knowledge itself. Let the methods and the subjects be appropriate for the ages of the pupils, and their love of learning will continue.

7. The steps in learning should not be too great. If a desire for knowledge is to be maintained, the pupil must be able to see clearly how one portion of a subject is connected with another. The step to be taken should be based on those already established, and the teacher should remember that what appears but a mole hill to him may be a mountain to his pupils. He is the best teacher who can most clearly remember his own early difficulties in learning.

8. Lessons must not be too long. This is true, both as regards lessons at school and those assigned for home preparation. Long-continued lessons in school weary the mind; long lessons learned at home tire both mind and body. When learning becomes a "task" it necessarily ceases to be attractive in itself. It should not be surprising that under such circumstances children lose their natural eagerness for knowledge.

If the suggestions given be carried out in the right spirit, boys and girls will continue to be "interrogative machines" throughout their whole lives.

CHAPTER VII.

HOW TO GRATIFY AND DEVELOP THE NATURAL DESIRE FOR MENTAL ACTIVITY.

Activity is one of the instincts of childhood. It is not happy unless its mental or physical powers or both are engaged. "*Productive activity*" is the corner stone of the delightful and truly philosophical system of Froebel. Give a child work to do of a character suited to his age, let it call his mental faculties and manual abilities into play, and he will be *attentive*, not merely because he is occupied, but because his occupation gives him delight. Fellenberg says: "Experience has taught me that *indolence* in young persons is so directly opposite to their natural disposition to activity, that unless it is the consequence of bad education, it is almost invariably connected with some constitutional defect." Hailman says: "Perhaps attention and activity of the mind are convertible terms; for we observe that the mind is never attentive, unless it is aroused to action by some external cause (such as a wonderful object, an exciting scene, a thrilling narrative, a deep sorrow), or by an internal cause—the will." It is important, therefore, in order to secure attention, that every means be taken to awaken and satisfy the child's *mental activity*. To do this it will be found necessary to attend to the following :—

1. Do as little telling as possible when teaching. Of course, the teacher should not try to teach everything by experiment, as he would waste time in doing so. The accumulated knowledge of the ages is a store from which the pupils ought to be allowed to draw largely without making all the necessary discoveries and progressive steps themselves. But whenever the teacher can *lead* his pupils in the development of a subject he should do so. He should not allow them to wander in search of the gold mines of knowledge, neither should he dig the gold and coin it for them. The word for "schoolmaster" in the Welsh language has a very suggestive meaning. The word for school is 'Ysgol," which conveys the meaning at once of progression in learning being step by step, commencing at the lowest rung and going upwards. The Welsh name for schoolmaster is " Ysgolfeister," the full signification being " One that teaches to climb." The teacher should not merely climb himself and throw down to his pupils the treasures which he finds. He should teach each pupil to climb for himself, so that as he goes higher he may grow stronger. "This need for perpetual *telling* is the result of our stupidity, not the child's. We drag it away from the facts in which it is interested, and which it is actively assimilating for itself; we put before it facts far too complex for it to understand, and therefore distasteful to it; finding that it will not voluntarily acquire these facts, we thrust them into its mind by force of threats and punishment; by thus denying it the knowledge it craves, and cramming it with knowledge it cannot digest, we produce a morbid state of the faculties, and a consequent disgust for knowledge in general; and when, as a result partly of the stolid indolence we have brought on, and partly of still continued unfitness in its studies, the child can understand nothing without explanation, and becomes a mere passive recipient of our instruction, we infer that education must necessarily be carried on thus. Having by our method induced helplessness, we straightway make the helplessness a reason for our method." *

2. Give the pupils their rightful share in the work of study.

Too much dependence is placed in eye teaching by many teachers. The observant faculties are certainly of great importance, and the teacher who develops them to a high degree will be well repaid for his trouble. Pupils may *see* a great deal without receiving fixed impressions however. Seeing does not require intensity of attention. The teacher cannot always be certain that the *looking* child is thinking about the subject in hand. He may look at the teacher, or the blackboard, or an object and yet be thinking about his last fishing experience.

To require each pupil to do for himself, is the only way of absolutely compelling him to attend. It is not receiving knowledge that fixes it in the minds of pupils, but reproducing it. If it can be reproduced by the hand in a visible form, the attention is necessarily most continuous. The mind must attend, if it has to guide the hand.

---

* Intellectual Education.—*Herbert Spencer.*

Each pupil should *do* for himself the map his teacher draws on the board, he must *do* the correction of his own mistakes; and if he is made to *do* work with his hands in learning any subject by even writing down the statements made concerning it, the impressions made will be more permanent than if made in any other way. The inattention so lamentably noticeable in most Sunday Schools, and many Public Schools, is due to the fact that pupils are mere recipients of information and not *active participators* in the process of learning. They are hearers, when they should be doers.

3. Do not weary the minds of the pupils.

A proper amount of physical exercise produces beneficial effects on the muscular system; beyond a certain point it is exhaustive. So a judicious amount of mental exercise strengthens and develops the mental powers, but study after the "fatigue point" has been reached has a debilitating effect. The moderate use of the physical powers gives pleasure, and increases the longing for exertion; so the judicious application of the mind awakens greater desire for study, and gives additional power to investigate the problems which may be presented for thought. Professor

Pillans held that, "where young people are taught as they ought to be, they are quite as happy in school as at play, seldom less delighted, nay, often more, with the well-directed use of their mental energies, than with that of their muscular powers."

4. Do not overload the minds of the pupils. The carrying power of a child's mind is frequently over-estimated by teachers. Many brilliant boys are made to carry such large loads of knowledge during their schooldays, that they become mentally paralyzed to a certain extent, and never recover their full vigor of thought. This partly accounts for the fact that so many clever school boys turn out to be only mediocre men. Over eating causes dyspepsia and destroys the appetite for food. There are mental dyspeptics.

5. Have matches in the various school subjects. Who does not remember the enlivening effects of the spelling matches of his boyhood? So intensely was their attention concentrated upon the subject in hand, that grown men remember distinctly the very words missed by themselves and others in some remarkable contests. Such matches may just as well be conducted in reviewing the other school subjects as in spelling, and their effects in inspiriting classes will always be found to be very beneficial. They should not be held at stated times, or conducted in a formal and indifferent manner by the teacher, or they will lose their interest.

6. Let pupils question each other. The contests which will awaken the highest degree of mental activity on the part of pupils are those conducted by themselves. Confine them to the work actually taught and give them due notice, and such exercises will produce the most satisfactory results. No other plan will set pupils to work for themselves more earnestly and intelligently. It is a good plan in some subjects to prepare a series of questions for the pupils covering the work to be learned. These should not be given that the pupils may merely prepare answers to them, to be recited in a parrot-like manner. They should simply guide to the golden thoughts. They may be of use also to the pupils in preparing for the contests recommended. Professor White, of Oberlin College, says: "The pupils of a certain high school failed to be instructed in 'The Science of Government,' in which weekly exercises had been given to them for nearly a whole term. In despair the principal wrote carefully 200 questions, covering the whole work. These he placed in the hands of each pupil, and dividing the whole school into two sides, allowed each in turn to question the other side till he obtained a satisfactory answer, while he sat by to watch the 'slaughter of the innocents.' The first exercise was a failure, seeming merely to arouse the school; the second was successful, and the fifth was brilliant."

7. Question while teaching. Some teachers only ask questions while reviewing. This is a serious mistake. To test knowledge is certainly one of the functions of questioning, but it is a subordinate one. Socratic, Instructive, Teaching, or Developing questioning is the most efficacious mode of teaching. It does not simply give information; it arouses the minds of pupils to activity, guides the active minds in the acquisition of knowledge, and sets the stored minds upon the plan of using the information obtained. It develops not only *receptive*, but *productive activity*. "He who gives knowledge to the human mind is a benefactor; but far greater is he who by giving knowledge quickens into activity and productiveness the mind upon which he works. The true teaching process involves the power of *intellectual quickening*, which is that process by which the teacher excites the intellectual powers of his pupils to self-activity in the line of his teaching; and to be really effective it must also lead to the courses of thought, feeling, purpose, and action which are the proper products of the truth taught."

Teachers should talk and tell less, and draw out more. Questioning from the known to the unknown welds the links in the chain of knowledge as they are formed, so that when completed they are not merely isolated facts. It gives a pupil a conscious power to show him that he can overcome difficulties for himself.

8. Use illustrations. There are several kinds of illustrations. The following should be largely used in teaching:

1. *Blackboard illustration.*
2. *Picture, map, and chart illustration.*
3. *Model illustration.*
4. *Object illustration.*
5. *Illustration by experiments.*
6. *Dramatic illustration.*

Blackboard illustration is of more use than any or perhaps all other kinds of illustration. Every teacher can use it; no teacher should try to teach without it. Its superiority over other methods of illustration consists chiefly in the fact that the work *grows* in the presence of the pupils. They see it made and help to make it, either by actually handling the crayon, or by making suggestions step by step as to what should be done next. The teacher who presents a finished illustration to his class weakens its effect by at least one half. It is nearly as bad to do the whole illustration, even in the presence of the pupils, without explanation to them, or assistance from them at every step. Some teachers work the complete solution of a problem on the board, when illustrating a new rule in arithmetic or algebra without speaking or even looking at the class until they have finished it. Then they turn round and give the explanation in the stereotyped question, " Do you see ? " They would have interested their pupils a great deal more, and have educated them nearly as much, by tossing a copper for " heads or tails." The following rules should be practised in blackboard illustration :

1. Let the work done be simple in its character.

2. Avoid symbolism, rebuses, &c.

3. Arrange the steps in the process of thought in logical order.

4. Number the various steps either by figures or letters.

5. The steps in the illustration should be done as the process of thought is developed.

6. When illustrating distinctive characteristics, peculiarities of growth or construction, &c., in teaching botany, zoology, natural philosophy,&c., it is well to exaggerate the special parts to which attention should be directed.

7. In solving a problem, making a diagram, drawing a map, explaining the construction of a machine, in fact in all kinds of blackboard work, every pupil ought to do on slate or paper what the teacher does on the board, and usually part by part after him.

2. Picture, map, and chart illustration may be used in conjunction with blackboard illustration, both preceding and following it, to give a correct idea of things as *wholes*, and to shew in some cases the coloring, &c. They ought to be used too in testing the accuracy of the work done by the teacher and pupils. For instance, when a map has been sketched it should be compared in its leading outlines with the actual map to see whether the great features bear their proper relations to each other; whether Florida extends further south than California,&c.

3. Model illustration is used by some teachers very successfully by cutting out the shapes of things or their parts from brown paper, &c. Models of machines, of the parts of the human frame, &c., may be obtained, which will be of great use in teaching some subjects. Good teachers, however, usually try to make most of their own models.

4. In Object illustration the pupils should not merely *look at* the things used. They should take them in their hands and examine them. This will enable them to get additional ideas through the sense of touch, and will clearly define those received by looking at the object at a distance. It will also give them a deeper interest in the object to be permitted to handle it. It is sometimes well to state the nature of the information desired before passing an object around, but frequently the pupils should be required to examine specimens with the view of finding out as much as possible about them. This will make them independent observers.

5. Illustration by experiment should as far as possible be conducted on the same principles as object illustration. It produces its highest results when every student performs for himself the experiments described by the teacher. If this cannot be done, the pupils, unless the class be too large, should assist the teacher, each taking some part in preparing for the experiment.

6. Dramatic illustration means representation by action. The living, energetic teacher uses this method of illustration very largely, and if appropriate it always aids greatly in communicating knowledge. It is of much use in giving ideas of shape, size, direction, motion, action of machines, &c. Any one who has ever seen a deaf mute address an audience by *signs*, must have realized to what an extent action may be even substituted for speech. A good teacher always uses his hands and arms to emphasize, and illustrate what he says to his class.

DEVELOPING MENTAL ACTIVITY.

In all kinds of illustration it is well to keep the pictures, charts, maps, models, objects, apparatus, &c., out of sight as much as possible until the time arrives for using it. This stimulates the curiosity of the pupils and prevents the distraction of their attention. To show pictures at once, or to present the spectacle of a table covered with apparatus is a capital method of gaining attention to the pictures or apparatus. It may make it all the more difficult, however, on this account to get the attention concentrated on the lesson itself.

CHAPTER VIII.

CULTIVATION OF THE SENSES.

"Attention to the *external* is called observation, to the *internal* reflection." It is of the highest importance that the senses be trained so that they may be able to perform properly the various functions required of them through life. We should not aim at an impossible standard, or strive only to develop acuteness of the senses. Alertness is also required. Sharpness of vision will be of no service if the eyes are kept closed; acuteness of hearing will do little good unless the mind is in a receptive attitude. The telephonic circuit must be established before the hearing produces impressions on the brain. Pestalozzi held that, "Observation is the basis of all knowledge. The first object, then, in education must be to lead the child to observe with accuracy."

We should aim, then, to make the senses

>Attentive.
>
>Acute.
>
>Alert.
>
>Accurate.

How can this be done?

1. By Object Lessons. The three rules for the development of the senses are, 1st exercise them, 2nd *exercise them*, 3rd EXERCISE THEM. Well conducted object lessons will give an opportunity for the required exercise better than any other school subject. Unfortunately what are called "object lessons" are commonly used merely for the purpose of giving information, rather than to develop the power of acquiring it. Object lessons should not be statements of facts concerning the objects used. The information may be valuable, but in true object teaching it occupies a secondary or incidental place. The great aim, indeed the only aim of the teacher should be to present a well selected system of objects to the pupils, about which they may exercise their senses. Lessons on "common things" may be taught, and if taught they should as far as possible be taught objectively, but lessons on "common things" are no more true "object lessons" than lessons in Geography, History, or Grammar. Arithmetic, Geometry, Natural Philosophy, Chemistry, Natural History and Botany when properly taught are true object lessons. Lessons on common things intended to convey information concerning the source, growth, production, &c., of the things used in every-day life are not object lessons. However valuable or practical the information may be, if the teacher contents himself with merely storing his pupils' minds with it he is lamentably failing to perform his true duty. However able the teacher may be, the shortness of the time during which most children attend school, prevents his giving information in regard to the greater portion of the vast field of knowledge. Hailman says: "There must be a systematic "laying up" of positive information, but this is of secondary importance, compared with *learning how to form and express* ideas.

One is the ability to work, the other the result of work, one is essential the other a consequence, one is constant, the same at all times and under all circumstances, the latter must change with time and circumstances." The teacher's duty is to continue the educative process begun by nature before the school period, and to send a pupil to the world again at the conclusion of his school life fully prepared to continue under all circumstances and at all times the process of self-education. The faculties which the child has on entering school should not merely be filled with information they should be nourished and strengthened. The teacher's aim in teaching should be first to develop, second to store the mind with knowledge. This is true of all subjects, but especially of object lessons. Object lessons should be given in teaching nearly every subject, however. The *name* " Object Lesson" is misleading, as it restricts broad principles to one comparatively unimportant department of school work. Many speakers on educational topics speak as though developing or intuition teaching was only to be practised while teaching object lessons. No greater error could be made. But even in " giving" an object lesson many teachers seem to regard the giving of mere facts as the great aim to be kept in view. Perhaps the most ridiculous feature of such object teaching is the fact, that teachers usually select for their lessons some common objects, with which the pupils are quite as well acquainted as they are themselves. It is right to select common objects for proper "object lessons," but not for *information exercises*.

The books on object teaching are to blame for much of the misunderstanding in reference to this subject. They are mere compendiums of information. They give *matter* not *method*. "The intention of object lessons is not so much to communicate information as to put children in the way of collecting information for themselves; to sharpen and direct their senses; to teach them to see things, instead of merely looking at them, and to decompose the confused aggregate of impressions which things at first make upon the mind; to get them to classify and connect simple phenomena with their antecedents and consequents; to exercise their reason; and to do this in Nature's own way, by bringing the learner, as far as possible into direct contact with things, and satisfying his own instinctive needs."

In teaching object lessons the following rules should be observed:

1. Let every pupil have the opportunity of examining the object.

2. Let the pupils examine first with a view of finding out as much as possible about the object themselves.

3. Let them, if necessary, then inspect it for specific results named by the teacher.

They should be independent of the teacher in making their observations, as they will have to depend on themselves after they leave school, therefore the first method of inspection should be most regularly used.

2. Reading. By true Object lessons all the senses may be developed. The two senses which teachers should specially aim to cultivate are hearing and seeing. "The defects in organization are not within the power of the preceptor; but we may observe that inattention and want of exercise are frequently the causes of what are mistaken for natural defects; and, on the contrary, increased attention and cultivation sometimes produce that quickness of eye and ear, and that consequent readiness of judgment, which we are apt to attribute to natural superiority of organization or capacity."

For rendering the hearing acute and *alert* there is no subject on the school programme of such importance as reading, if it is properly taught.

There is a great deal of telling done improperly in the teaching of reading. When a pupil has finished his reading the teacher usually at once proceeds to *tell* him the mistakes he has made. "You should say re-cess', instead of *re'-cess*, catch instead of *ketch*, get instead of *git;* you should not pause after in; you should pause after *March;* you should emphasize *dying*, &c., &c." That this is a mistake will at once be seen, when it is remembered that correct reading and speaking depend upon ear cultivation more than on anything else. The great majority of people do not perceive, when they hear a word pronounced in a manner different from the way in which they are accustomed to pronounce it themselves. Unless some one calls attention to their errors, they go on mispro-

CULTIVATION OF THE SENSES. 69

nouncing words, which they hear pronounced correctly every day. This result should be expected, if pupils are corrected in the above manner throughout their school life.

When a mistake is made in pronunciation, accent, emphasis, pauses, intonation, &c., the teacher should give the correct reading himself, or get one of the best pupils to do so, and call on the pupil who made the error to state the difference between his reading and that of his teacher. If he cannot do so, it is useless to ask him to "read it again" as is frequently done. The teacher should read the sentence, or that portion in which the error is made, in both the correct and the incorrect way, emphasizing the error slightly if necessary, until the pupil can distinguish the one method from the other. In this way the ear will become quickened and attentive, and the pupil will be self-educative in this respect, as he should be in all others, when he leaves school.

The seeing power may also be developed in a high degree by reading. The vision must be acute to read well. Every letter in every word must be looked at, and yet the perceptions must be sharp and clearly defined. To many pupils when learning the words appear indistinct, as they look to one reading in a faint light. This must be remedied by practice. It will not help the pupil to see accurately, if the mis-named words are corrected by the teacher. If the pupil, for instance, reads *verily*, *very*, and the teacher merely says, as most teachers do, "Call that word *very*," the pupil's vision is not rendered more sharp. When mis-calling words is the only mistake made or the special one to be corrected, the best method the teacher can adopt is to say, "Read again carefully." The pupil can correct his own mistakes in this case, and he should be made to do so.

3. Spelling. While both the eye and the ear can be developed by means of spelling, it is mainly through the former that we must teach this subject. Good spelling depends on the "memory of the eye." *The London Times* once said, "Spelling is learnt by reading, and nothing but reading can teach spelling." Spelling depends on the *intensity of the attention* with which pupils look at words and their parts while reading them. If teachers can succeed in developing the habit of close and accurate scrutiny of the letters in the words during reading lessons, they will have little bad spelling. Careless readers are inaccurate spellers. The eye has to look at each individual letter on a page as it is read. Attention then cannot be *snstained*, as the glance at each letter must be instantaneous. It should, however, be *intense*, and, as most words recur frequently, it will be oft *repeated*. On the intensity and repetition of attention depend the accuracy and the permanence of impressions, so that if they can be secured the best results must follow in teaching any subject. In regard to spelling, the teacher has only to secure the intenssity, except in the case of words that but rarely appear in print. If the necessary interest cannot be aroused in reading to secure a sufficient degree of attention to the words as they are read, the teacher must have recourse to other methods which will compel the required attention. The best way of doing this is to make pupils write out the spelling lesson. It is surprising that many pupils will at first make mistakes even in transcription. As they can be held responsible for the use of their eyes, however, they will soon learn by practice to see accurately and copy correctly. When a pupil is required to write several times a word which he has mis-spelled, it is not with a view of making him *think* how the word is spelled, but to help him to *see* the letters it contains, and how they are arranged. The practice is based upon the sound principle that actual *doing* is the best means of compelling attention to any subject.

4. Drawing. Drawings are executed with the hand, the hand is guided by the brain, and the brain receives its impressions about the lines to be drawn through the senses. This is an explanation of the general principle laid down in the last paragraph, that doing with the hand compels attention. If the sense impressions are inaccurate the hand can not be definitely guided. In most kinds of drawing the eye is the medium through which the mind obtains the ideas which the hand is to reproduce on paper. The eye therefore usually has two functions in regard to this subject:

1. To receive exact impressions of the copy or object to be drawn.

2. To inspect the drawing as it is being executed to see that it is correctly done.

There is no subject on the school programme which compels attention on the part of all pupils to a greater extent than *Dictation* drawing. The terms used are so definite in their meaning that the slightest misconception of the teacher's language, when dictating forms and their combinations, will show itself in an incorrect picture. Every pupil must therefore give close attention in this subject or his negligence will be detected.

5. Writing. The remarks made about the use of the eye in drawing from copies on paper, on the blackboard, or from objects, apply also to writing, if it is properly taught. The eye should carefully analyze the letter to be written, and inspect the written letter with the view of finding out by comparison with the copy what its defects are. Unfortunately too many teachers prevent this inspection by the pupils by pointing out the errors made, instead of merely directing attention to them, so that the pupils might discover their nature for themselves and thus become in this, as they should ultimately become in all subjects, independent of the teacher.

6. Hints. There are some special exercises

for the development of the ability to see and hear. For instance a picture may be shown for only a few seconds to a class and then each pupil allowed to describe something that he saw in it; or various noises may be made by striking different substances and otherwise, in the hearing but not within the sight of the pupils, that they may form opinions as to the causes of the various sounds produced.

Notes on a musical instrument should be sounded at random until each pupil could recognize them unerringly as they are given. Other exercises of a similar nature will suggest themselves to teachers. They may take the form of games to relieve the wearisomeness or the monotony of school work.

CHAPTER IX.

GENERAL SUGGESTIONS.

1. Get the sympathy of your class. If your pupils are interested in you, they can be more easily interested by you in their lessons. The love of approbation is a strong motive, if the teacher is liked by the pupils. The desire to please a kind teacher will lead to great efforts to concentrate the attention on the subject he teaches. Teachers should strive to be cheerful, kind, courteous, polite, and discriminating in all their intercourse with their pupils in and out of school. "Good mornings" are easily given, but not easily forgotten.

2. Get the confidence of your class. Let them see not merely that you regard the subjects you teach as of great importance, but also that you arouse no inquiring interest whose questions you cannot answer. Be prepared with your work. Acknowledge frankly your lack of information in regard to any question which comes up unexpectedly and which you have not before considered. If you do so your pupils will have implicit faith in you, when you assume to speak definitely.

3. Be magnetic. It is not enough to merely attract a pupil's attention, it must be *held*. The teacher's manner has a good deal to do with holding the attention of his class. He should for the time, make the pupils forget their individual personality, and become one in aim and purpose with himself. How can this be done?

1. The teacher must understand his subject and have his lesson arranged so that he is not conscious of mental strain in teaching it.

2. He must believe his lesson to be important.

3. He must be earnest and enthusiastic, in order to stir up a corresponding zeal on the part of his pupils.

4. He must not be listless, cold, formal, or mechanical in his teaching.

4. Appeal to the natural instincts of a child. The following should be used as incentives to attention:—

1. *Curiosity.* The desire to know, the inquisitive faculty that worries busy mothers, and, in too many homes and schools, dies from lack of exercise and nourishment.

2. *Love of activity.* Mental activity gives quite as much delight to a healthy child as physical exercise. Neither affords pleasure, if it degenerates into drudgery. There are few boys who appreciate very highly the privilege of digging ditches day after day. Mental ditching is no more attractive to them.

3. *Sympathy.* This leads to unity of purpose and co-operation between teacher and pupils. They should get out of their own channels of thought and into his, for the time being. It is clear that the broader and deeper his channel is,

the more easily his pupils may get into it, and the more rapid will be their progress in it.

4. *Love of praise.* If the pupil has the proper amount of respect for his teacher, he will be very desirous of earning his approbation. Teachers should not be too sparing in their commendation of earnest efforts. Praise for honest work.

5. *Fear of offending.* The pupil who loves his teacher will endeavor to avoid causing him annoyance, and will be glad to learn his lessons or give attention, if he can save his teacher pain by doing so.

6. *Emulation.* While too great a rivalry is likely to produce evil results that may outweigh the good done, it is well to use, as a motive power, as much of the spirit of emulation as will awaken increased interest, and arouse to energetic work.

7. *Appreciation of resulting benefits.* As pupils grow older, they should be led to take an interest in study for its ultimate aims, developing character, and fitting for usefulness in the various walks of life.

5. Think out each lesson for yourself. Do not merely memorize lessons, or depend upon those prepared by others, however good they may be. Let the lesson become your own by a careful process of thought, let this process be repeated until it has become fixed, and your personal, magnetic power will be increased very largely. There is as much difference in the personal influence of a teacher whose lesson has been thought out, and that of one whose lesson has been learned by rote, as there is between the attractiveness of an orator who speaks without notes, and the man who reads his sermons or speeches.

The one teacher can give his attention to his class, the other must attend to his lesson, lest he may forget it.

The difference in the effect produced by the two ways of teaching is much greater with children than with adults.

6. Use the pupils' eyes. If the interest is beginning to flag, show the pupils something. Illustrate the work in some way, even if you have to change the designed order of your lesson to make the illustration appropriate. The teacher who only *talks* to his class, uses only half his teaching power, and employs less than half of the receptive power of the pupils. It is often a good way to begin with an illustration, so as to concentrate the attention at once upon the subject in hand, and drive out the thoughts which have been occupying the minds of the scholars.

7. Give occasional rests. Giving fixed and intense attention is an exhaustive effort. Rest does not necessarily mean cessation from effort. Relief may be given to one faculty by the exercise of another. Variety is in many cases equivalent to rest.

8. Do not distract attention. It is wrong to stop the work of a whole class to scold one pupil for inattention, or even to notice his listlessness in such a way as to disconcert others. A question will be sufficient to arrest and reprove him. " Teachers themselves often distract the attention of children by the injudicious way in which they handle a subject ; by importing into their lesson irrelevant matter ; by mixing up information that ought to be kept distinct; by a see-saw mode of procedure; by exhibiting pictures, specimens, etc., before they are required, and by leaving them before the class after they have served their purpose.

9. Do not be discouraged if children at first have difficulty in giving fixed attention. It is hard work to give continued attention. The teacher should develop the power gradually at first. Currie expresses this idea well. He says, " The power of attention is the result of habit. Time must therefore be allowed for its growth. The first efforts exacted from the child should be gentle; one point should be presented at a time, that he may not be bewildered by multiplicity; the strain on his attention should not be long continued; he should be relieved before he is compelled to desist from fatigue; one success will make a subsequent one easier of attainment; failure will make the next attempt more arduous."

10. Use judgment in questioning. The following rules concerning questioning have special reference to securing attention :—

1. Do not ask questions in *rotation*.

2. Do not *point* to the pupil whom you wish to answer while asking a question.

3. Do not even *look* fixedly at the pupil whom you wish to answer, while giving the question.

4. State questions to the class as a *whole;* ask one member for the answer.

5. Do not wait an instant for the answer when *reviewing* most subjects.

6. Do not look steadily at the pupil who is answering.

7. Do not *repeat* a question to oblige those who were inattentive.

8. Be sure to ask questions to those who are in the *slightest degree inattentive.*

11. Do not depend too much on simultaneous answering. If you do, you cannot be sure that your pupils are giving intelligent attention. They may join mechanically in repeating an answer without thinking. Pupils may be taught to speak out by simultaneous answering, and time may sometimes be saved by its use. Simultaneous repetition and simultaneous answering must not be confounded. The frequent repetition of anything to be learned by rote is often the quickest and surest way of impressing it on the minds of pupils. All the members of a class if well trained, may responsively repeat brief statements made by the teacher while teaching. They may even answer together when being reviewed, if the teacher wishes the answer to be given in a set form of words. Even then there is a danger that the indolent will wait for the keynotes from the leaders. They should never answer together while being taught, unless their answers can be given by a single word. If the answer to a question requires independent thought, and it is of little consequence unless it does so, it should not be answered simultaneously, as each pupil may have a different answer. If the answers are certain to be literally the same they may be given at the same time. Even simultaneous repetition requires great care. The teacher must speak with the greatest possible precision and distinctness, and he must listen with the utmost care to the responses made. These responses should be given in a natural tone of voice. *Classes* that are allowed to repeat together are liable to acquire a loud drawling manner of speaking that is very disagreeable. Every teacher should remember, however, that in its most perfect form *simultaneous answering is the most mechanical kind of teaching.* It is *word grinding*, and generally the words even if correctly uttered form but an " unmeaning jargon " to the pupils.

Many very ludicrous examples might be given to show that children do not even get the right words when taught to repeat in concert.

A girl who had learned in this way to repeat Byron's lines on the Battle of Waterloo, grew to be a woman with the impression that one line read :

Ah Marm, it is, it is the cannons' opening roar.

Sunday school children frequently make dreadful parodies of the hymns taught to them.

The following answers were given by pupils eleven years of age in one of the schools of London, England. They had been accustomed to repeat the catechism half an hour of each day in day school and in Sunday school for four or five years, and this is what they wrote:

"My duty toads God is to bleed in him to fering and to loaf withold your arts withold my mine withold my sold and with my sernth to whirchp and to give thanks to put my old trast in him to call upon him to onner his old name and his world and to save him truly all the days of my life's end.

My dooty tords by nabers to love him as thyself and to do to all men as I wed thou shall do and to me to love onner and suke my farther and mother and bey the queen and all that are pet in a forty under her to smit myself to all my goones teachers spartial pastures and masters who oughten myself lordly and every to all my betters to hut nobody by would nor deed to be trew and jest in all deelins to beer no malis nor ated in your arts to kep my ands from pecking and steel my turn from evil speak and lawing and slanders not to civit or desar othermans good but to lern labour trewly to get my own leaving and to do my dooty in that state if life and to each it hes please God to call men."

Another gave the following answer to the question "Who was Moses?"

"He was an Egypshin. He lived in a bark maid of bull rushers and he kep a golden calf and worship braizen snakes and he het nuthin but kwales and manner for forty year. He was kort by the air of his ed while riding under the bow of a tree and he was killed by his Abslon as he was a hanging from the bow. His end was pease."

Do not be deceived. Simultaneous answering is not a developing exercise. The very pupils who should attend most carefully, often do not attend at all, when this method is adopted.

TEACHERS' PROFESSIONAL WORKS.

WORKS BY DR. McLELLAN.

McLellan and Kirkland's Examination Papers in Arithmetic............................... 1 00

A complete series of Problems, designed for use in Schools and Colleges, and especially adapted for the preparation of Candidates for Teachers' Certificates, by J. A. McLellan, M.A., LL.D., Inspector of High Schools, and Thomas Kirkland, M.A., Science Master Normal School, Toronto. 6th Edition—revised.

McLellan and Kirkland's Examination Papers—Part I.................................. 0 50

Containing the Examination Papers for admission to High Schools, and for Candidates for Third Class Teachers' Certificates.

Hints and Answers to McLellan and Kirkland's Examination Papers 1 00

Containing answers to problems and solutions to all difficult questions. Prepared by the authors. 2nd Edition.

The leading American Educational Journal (*National Teacher's Monthly*) says of McLellan and Kirkland's Examination Papers: "In our opinion, the best collection of problems on the American continent."

McLellan's Mental Arithmetic—Part I........... 0 30

Containing the Fundamental Rules, Fractions and Analysis. By J. A. McLellan, M.A., LL.D., Inspector of High Schools, Ontario. 3rd Edition.

McLellan's Mental Arithmetic—Part II. 0 45

By the same author, fully treats Percentage in its various applications, General Analysis, Stocks and Shares, Interest, Discount, etc., etc., and gives practical solutions of almost every type of question likely to be met with in any treatise on Arithmetic. 3rd Edition—revised.

TEACHERS' PROFESSIONAL WORKS.

THE TEACHER'S HAND-BOOK OF ALGEBRA.

By J. A. McLELLAN, M.A., LL.D., Inspector of High Schools, Ontario. Price, $1.25.

The Hand-book contains over 2,500 Exercises, including about 350 Solved Examples, illustrating every type of question in Elementary Algebra.

It contains complete explanation of Horner's Multiplication and Division, with application not given in the Text Books.

It contains a more complete illustration of the Theory of Divisors, with its beautiful applications, than is to be found in any Text Book.

It contains what able Mathematical Teachers have pronounced to be the "finest chapter on factoring that has ever appeared."

It contains the "finest selection of properly classified Equations, with methods of resolution and reduction, that has yet appeared."

It contains a set of Practice Papers, made up by selecting the best of the questions set by the University of Toronto during twenty years.

It is a Key of Methods, a Repertory of Exercises, which cannot fail to make the teacher a better teacher, and the student a more thorough algebraist.

Most excellent manual.—*Ohio Educational Journal.*

Its Author.—It is the work of one of the first mathematicians in the country. It should be in the hands of every teacher.—*British Whig, Kingston.*

Best Algebra published.—*News, Kingston.*

Useful to teachers who desire to obtain a thorough grasp of the subject, and to learners who wish to make preparation for an extended course of algebraic study.—*Maryland School Journal (Hon. M. A. Newell, State Supt. of Education, Editor.*

Compact and Useful.—*School Bulletin, Syracuse, N.Y.*

A capital volume, and prepared by one who understands his business.—*New York School Journal.*

A useful supplement to the text books in common use.—*School Guardian, England.*

A valuable work for Teachers.—*Barnes' Educational Monthly.*

"The best algebra for teachers I have ever seen."—*From one of the greatest authorities on the subject in the United States, Dr. Stringham, John Hopkins University, Baltimore.*

Key to Hand-book of Algebra—2nd Edition 1 50

THE TEACHER'S HAND-BOOK OF ALGEBRA.

By J. A. McLELLAN, M.A., LL.D., Inspector of High Schools, Ontario. Price, $1.25.

ENGLAND.

No better proof of the excellence of this book can be given than the following quotation from the *Educational Times*, the organ of the College of Preceptors, England, and the highest authority on educational matters in Great Britain:—

"This is the work of a Canadian Teacher and Inspector, whose name is honorably known beyond the bounds of his native province, for his exertions in developing and promoting that admirable system of public instruction, which has placed the Dominion of Canada so high, as regards education, not only among the British Colonies, but among the civilized nations of the world. We know of no work in this country that exactly occupies the place of Dr. McLellan's, which is not merely a text book of Algebra, in the ordinary sense, but a Manual of Methods for Teachers, illustrating the best and most recent treatment of algebraical problems and solutions of every kind.

"Teachers who wish to lay a good foundation for their pupils before proceeding to the higher branches of Mathematics, will do well to obtain Dr. McLellan's volume, which contains within a small compass one of the best collections of modern algebraical problems 'gathered from the works of the great masters of analysis,' which has come under our notice for a considerable time."

FRANCE.

From one of the ablest living Mathematicians, Monsieur Paul Mansion, Professor of Mathematics in the University of Ghent, Assistant-Editor of "Nouvelle Correspondence Mathematique," and Editor in Chief of "Mathises," &c. His writings have twice been crowned by the Royal Academy of Belgium, and he was awarded, in 1872, Great Prize in Mathematical Science. He says of the Hand-Book:—"I have found the Work of M. McLellan extremely well adapted to its purpose. It is one of those rare works that fulfil all the promises of the preface. I have especially admired the skilful way in which he has brought within the compass of Elementary Algebra a class of questions, which we, in our French and German books, only introduce into the parts exclusively taught in Universities."

New and Revised Edition of Key to Handbook, now ready. Price, $1.50.

TEACHERS' PROFESSIONAL WORKS.

MISTAKES IN TEACHING.
By J. LAUGHLIN HUGHES, Supt. Public Schools, Toronto.

Second Edition. Price 50 Cents.

This work discusses, in a terse manner, over one hundred of the mistakes commonly made by untrained or inexperienced teachers. The mistakes are arranged under the following heads:

1. MISTAKES IN MANAGEMENT. 2. MISTAKES IN DISCIPLINE. 3. MISTAKES IN METHODS. 4. MISTAKES IN MANNER.

We advise every teacher to invest fifty cents in the purchase of this useful volume.—*New England Journal of Education.*

It contains good sense and wise counsel to teachers. All young teachers will find the book a help in their work—one of the best to be had.—*Educational Weekly, Chicago.*

For young teachers I know of no book that contains in the same compass so much matter directly bearing on their work, and capable of being immediately utilized.—HON. M. A. NEWELL, *State Superintendent of Education, in Maryland School Journal.*

Eminently practical. Most readable book for teachers that we have seen lately.—*Teacher's Advocate, Pa.*

We know of no book of the size that contains so many valuable suggestions for teachers, young or old.—*Educational Journal of Virginia.*

It contains more hints of practical value to teachers than any book of its size known to us.—*Ohio Educational Monthly.*

It might with profit be read aloud at teachers' meetings everywhere, in fact it is a sort of Teachers' Looking Glass.—*Barnes' Educational Monthly.*

We know of no book containing more valuable suggestions to teachers.—*Central School Journal, Iowa.*

It is sensible and practical.—*School Bulletin, Syracuse, N.Y.*

TEACHERS' PROFESSIONAL WORKS.

The Canada School Journal
HAS RECEIVED
An Honorable Mention at Paris Exhibition, 1878.

Recommended by the Minister of Education, Ont.
Recommended by the Council of Public Instruction, Que.
Recommended by Chief Supt. of Education, N. B.
Recommended by Chief Supt. of Education, N. S.
Recommended by Chief Supt. of Education, B. C.
Recommended by Chief Supt. of Education, Man.

THE CANADA SCHOOL JOURNAL
IS EDITED BY

A Committee of some of the Leading Educationists in Ontario, assisted by able Provincial Editors in the Provinces of Quebec, Nova Scotia, New Brunswick, Prince Edward Island, Manitoba and British Columbia, thus having each section of the Dominion fully represented.

Contains Twenty-four pages of Reading Matter

Live Editorials; Contributions on important Educational topics; Selections—Readings for the School Room; and Notes and News from each Province.

PRACTICAL DEPARTMENT will always contain useful hints on methods of teaching different subjects.

MATHEMATICAL DEPARTMENT gives solutions to difficult problems also on Examination Papers.

OFFICIAL DEPARTMENT contains such regulations as may be issued from time to time.

Subscription, $1.00 *per annum, strictly in advance.*

A Club of 1,000 Subscribers from Nova Scotia.

EDUCATION OFFICE,
(Copy) HALIFAX, N.S., Nov. 16, 1878.
Messrs. ADAM MILLER & CO., Toronto, Ont.

DEAR SIRS,—In order to meet the wishes of our teachers in various parts of the Province, and to secure for them the advantage of your excellent periodical, I hereby subscribe in their behalf for one thousand (1,000) copies at club rates mentioned in your recent esteemed favor. Subscriptions will begin with January issue, and lists will be forwarded to your office in a few days.

Yours truly,
DAVID ALLISON, *Chief Supt. of Education.*

Address, **W. J. GAGE & CO.**, Toronto, Canada.

Gage's School Examiner

AND

Monthly Review

Of Science, Literature and Current Events.

A Magazine for the School Room and Study, containing

EXAMINATION PAPERS

on the subjects taught in the High and Public Schools, and designed for the use of Teachers in conducting Monthly Examinations, and in the daily work of the School Room, and for the use of Students preparing for the *Intermediate and all Official* Examinations.

In addition to *Original Papers prepared by Specialists* on the various subjects, valuable selections will be made from the University, High School and Public School Examinations in Europe and America, as well as from Normal School and other Examinations for Teachers, both Professional and Non-Professional.

The Magazine will also contain in a brief and readable form a comprehensive

RECORD OF THE WORLD'S WORK

for the month; designed to furnish Teacher's, Students and General Readers with a well-digested summary of what is worth remembering in connection with

Literature, Science and Current Events.

Issued 15th of each Month.

Subscription, $1.00 per year—payable in advance.

ADDRESS—W. J. GAGE & CO., Toronto, Canada.

www.ingramcontent.com/pod-product-compliance
Lightning Source LLC
Chambersburg PA
CBHW032239080426
42735CB00008B/923